BOA
EDITIONS
LIMITED

I Have Tasted the Apple

Poems by

Mary Crow

❦

BOA Editions, Ltd. ❦ Brockport, NY ❦ 1996

Copyright © 1996 by Mary Crow
All rights reserved
Manufactured in the United States of America

LC #: 95-83235
ISBN: 978-1-880238-33-2

For information about permission to reuse any material
from this book, please contact The Permissions Company at
www.permissionscompany.com or e-mail permdude@gmail.com.

Publications by BOA Editions, Ltd.—a not-for-profit corporation under
section 501 (c) (3) of the United States Internal Revenue Code—are made
possible with the assistance of grants from the Literature Program of the
New York State Council on the Arts, the Literature Program of the National
Endowment for the Arts, the Lannan Foundation, as well as from the
Rochester Area Foundation Community Arts Fund administered by the
Arts & Cultural Council for Greater Rochester, the County of Monroe, NY,
and from many individual supporters.

Cover Art: "Apple Painting" by Martha Crow, courtesy of the artist
Cover Design: Daphne Poulin-Stofer
Author Photo: Derek Shoaff-Bembry
Interior Design and Typesetting: Richard Foerster
BOA Logo: Mirko

State of the Arts

NYSCA

BOA Editions, Ltd.
A. Poulin, Jr., Founder (1938–1996)
250 North Goodman Street, Suite 306
Rochester, NY 14607
www.boaeditions.org

NATIONAL
ENDOWMENT
FOR THE ARTS

for my sons,
David Woerner and Rob Woerner

❦

GIFT

A friend from the south
has sent me an apple
too beautiful
to eat right away.
I hold it in my hands:
It is heavy and round
like the Earth.

—Jorge Teillier

CONTENTS

PART IV

❦

I

THE TWINS VISIT A FARM

The heavy black bulk of the draft horse
lay in the heat, circled by lime. Too huge
to bury, it was left for flies, night animals.
We walked around the gleaming hill
of its flanks, the nostrils tulip-blue,
tiny terrain of the pink gums,
belly mushrooming sweetness.

Too timid to touch this mystery,
we were old enough to know
this was his final
beauty, this laying out
on meadow grass, beside aspen.

That very afternoon we had chased the Holsteins
home, their full udders sloshing
warm milk on us as they ran,
their gentle lowing a quiet happiness.

Elderberries and wild raspberries
had caught at our skirts
as we trotted toward the old farmhouse
where Mrs. Chesrown was scrubbing the milk buckets
in the hot sudsy water and the final light.

Sun glinting on a black coat:
twilight closing over earth,
a time of evening that pinches.
I glanced across at my pigtailed twin
as we re-entered the gate of the farmyard.

She had grown this summer and her knees
looked knobbier, her legs, gangly.
Her face said: You too, you too.

❦

AS IF

A bristlecone—spidery as the pines
in old Chinese scrolls—
has rooted itself into the rocks' crevice,
spilling a pool of shade so I can perch here
to wait for the black bear said to roam
after the red syrup
in hummingbird feeders.

I am wishing him here—
up the rocks in his rolling trot,
his fur silky as the musty
blackness last night
outside my window
I stared into so hard
I thought my body would follow my gaze,
floating up and out
and into a bear's world:
shadowed aspen groves
where I could hear a sound like the sea's,
a place where the odor of bear urine
would be a welcome sign
to tell me my clan:
I am wishing him here.

Standing on the shoulders of the scratchy hillside,
we could brood over star-trails,
shuffle our wordlessness
in perfect self-love.
We could sharpen our claws
against the silence

and set out, tree after tree, for the secret hive.
If. As if.
If only.

After his months
under the old snow,
my bear is rising rough-coated, flatfooted,
tottering in the cold cycle
of lull and struggle.
And I am here
caught in my human musk
and history.

An old brown cabin down the road
sports a weather vane I love:
a tin sea churns
as a silver moon drops into it
while an old clipper with white sails
heaves on the roiling water.
The vane swings back and forth,
the ship goes on
flinging its tiny anchor out.

❦

MATH CLASS

Somehow that shriveled arm
seemed the perfect arm
for tracing the odd shapes of geometry
in white on our black chalkboard
showing us a woman could do
this unwomanly thing
and sometimes a girl would let out a giggle
almost like a pig squeak
and our teacher would stop, chalk
in her lifted hand
and her back would stiffen
as she turned and glared at us

then returned
to tracing out her mysteries
we girls thought
meant math is for old maids
dries women out
so they can't want the only things
that seemed worth wanting—
happy grins in the hallways
and dark back seats where his warm breath
made the short hair on our napes stand up

and so we would come back to be scolded
and any boy in the class
knew better what any kind of triangle was
or how to add the sides up
into answers that were her kind
of "I do"

and some days she put the chalk
down on her desk
and told us how her father
scalded her with boiling water
and her arm contracted in its healing
but we barely listened

because a small white note was moving
across the room
toward the last seat by the window
and she didn't notice
since she was back at the blackboard
back at the numbers she loved
and we were girls
who knew nothing at all.

❦

MY EGYPT

Flaubert tells us he wore himself out
trying to imitate the cry of the camel,
rattle interrupted by a gargle;
he wanted to take it back with him.

And Kuchuk's bedbugs fascinated him,
their smell mingled with the scent
of her skin. I want, he told her,
a touch of bitterness in things.

Temples, sand dunes, the very Nile itself
made him lazy, and he wrote home:
"I think of nothing at all,
not even the elevated thoughts

one should have here
in the presence of ruins!"
He sent his letter, then went off
to visit Kuchuk of the long legs

again, wondering whether she felt
any pleasure since "undoubtedly"
her button had been circumcised
when she was a child.

I who have traveled to Egypt confess
I saw another country. In Cairo
a man followed me and I had to run;
a student in a packed bus rubbed his crotch

against me while I tried to twist away.
At night I couldn't leave my cheap hotel.
I sat in my room reflecting on the touch
of bitterness in things.

❦

HITCH HIKER AT A TRUCK STOP

The hitch hiker asks to look at
the palms of my cold hands
and thanks me for unfolding them
on the frost-edged
picnic table between us.
While I look at his downcast eyes
trying to see if he sees,
nearby truckers stare
at his narrow face,
long blonde hair.
He asks me if I garden,
rips a scrap of newspaper
and folds it up
into a tiny origami
package for anise seed.
Here, he says,
seed I gathered in Oregon,
plant it in Colorado.
I always have a garden, he adds,
I plant and leave to others.
He tells me he has no sex;
when you ride in the righthand seat,
you have to nod your head
without listening.
Face pressed to the window,
he can see the lacquered edges
of the earth.
So I imagine him
practicing calligraphy
on truck windows,

recommending honey and vinegar
in a glass of water
every morning.
Mad, mad, mad.
A yellow warbler,
the moon at the bottom of the stream.
Out on the highway
he is raising his thumb again.

❧

GYPSY IN CHINATOWN, LIMA, PERU

"The Heart is a female organ."
—Roland Barthes

Cross my palm, the gypsy said,
and the fire flashed
beneath the giant wok.
Waiters hustled bowls of noodles
over the littered floor
while the man across the table
kept warning me
of the dangers of streets,
sea-crossings, fortune tellers.
You need me,
he whispered.
Cross my palm, the gypsy said,
your hands are full of stories.
I folded the bill
and passed it to her
under the table.
Don't trust her,
the man was telling me,
don't give her anything.
You will find, she sighed,
someone better;
this one is evil—
watch out for him.
And her finger traced
my life line.
Here is: loneliness,
love, long life, travel.
You are young at heart,
she smiled, but this man

will make you old.
Your sea is pounding
on another shore.
The Chinese waiter
was speaking in Spanish,
Mas cerveza?
We ordered another round.
Sister, she said, I offer
friendship as well as fortune.
This man is dangerous.
Do not let him follow you.
You will wake
to find him barring
your way.
See how—as I speak—
in the map of your hand
your heart line
breaks into roads,
many roads.

❦

II

PRELUDE

"I can't stop thinking
about death," you wrote,
"so I want to hear about
the tilth of your days,
how you are making poetry."

"As usual," I answered,
"I am traveling. Some days
I can't remember where I am.
Here in Yugoslavia, they tell me,
acacia holds the world together."

I couldn't picture you
worrying about death:
Instead I remembered
how intently you used
to shop for dinner.

We would sit down to shrimps,
cauliflower and mayonnaise,
a crusty loaf,
golden red-cheeked mangoes.
You leaned across to kiss me.

Later, you'd put your arm
around my shoulders and ask me
question after question.
Slowly, slowly I entered the woods.
Slowly, I scattered the crumbs.

❧

GREEN WINE

Tomislav dom, near Zagreb

My new friend laughed as he leaned toward me,
over the litter of bread and half-empty glasses,
"The song is saying, 'I am sick with love,
and you are sick with love."'
Shrimp salad, risotto black with squid ink—
our feast lay in ruins before us
and down the table the drunken poet was moaning
about life's bitter dregs,
his wife so cruel she left him
taking his only child,
poetry no consolation.

But my friend and I rose to dance,
and followed the guitar and the banjo
as the singers circled the room
serenading their guests.

Wind banged the shutters and the barometer
was rising. All day the new green of spring
had quenched my body,
and now the wine looked green.

I could still taste the bread's salty crust
as I stepped into song. Who was this almost stranger
who had asked me to dance
by folding his hands as if in prayer
as he bowed his head

in my direction? Am I entering the real
country? Will his cheek taste bitter
or salt?

❧

ROUND

as red as to lose
and as round as to find
        —e. e. cummings

Trout leap from the Poudre River,
brief rosy flash, then the splash ripples
while I listen to you

as you twist the new ring you bought
because you couldn't stop touching
the empty place,

and you take it off and hand it to me.
New green lines the banks;
green bugs the trout desire

hover just out of reach.
I'm trying to leap
into what I need, letting my body

arch over the current
we're moving in, then drop,
staying with the must be,

with the big red oh
of the open mouth:
the muscular zero of it.

❦

PAST HISTORY

The red-headed basketball coach talked all class
about his wife,
handed out the tests: "Here, look it up."

So we spent fifth period
hunched over our history books,
eyes tracing the pages

for the facts,
minds on his words about what women want,
or at least what one woman wanted

but never got.
He dangled his long legs
over the desk's edge

while we perched like hungry cranes waiting for little fish,
beaks open.
Then he'd remember History and stop:

"Where were we?"
and would answer the silence, "Oh, yes,
Middle Ages."

I could feel the class hunker down
like the energy drop
when the house

lights jerk lower because evening demand
has made the power plummet.
I could see his thin wife

opening the front door
to greet him, apron still on,
left arm pushing back wisps of hair.

I tried to imagine
her turning
while she slowly unbuttoned

her housedress, but it was no good.
She was part of History,
and I wanted it

to be me, red dress tight, hair newly curled.
Surrender was feminine and the missionary
position best—that's

what he told us
as he leaned to look at the breasts of the girl in the first row.
Then he said we

had to wait till we married: our part of History.
Meanwhile, the red skirt
was lifting as my mind went blank:

all that dark sweatiness.

❦

A MOTHER'S INSOMNIA

after "Marching" by Charles Simic

"Then I rose in my house among my sons, . . ."
imagining their round faces turned up
like small moons toward the clouded sky.
I could not sleep because my eyes filled

with images of their marching all night,
the smell of wolves and snow on their boots.
The bodies of women bowed down before them
and old men trembled and knelt, villages

offered icons and candles to their ire.
Now I must go out into the garden to see
if my cabbages have wilted, to see
whether the cow is making sour milk.

Oh god, how that distant barking pierces
and I am afraid!
Not of my sons' dying, but of their living
like this: faces blank, their plump hands

little clouds folded over the fat earth
of their paunches, their irises bits of blue sky,
and over them a calm like the wind's aftermath
when only the smell remains.

❦

LAYERS

There is so much beneath this earth,
he was telling her. The farmers
furrow the soil and shards tumble out,
sometimes a skull. But it's not these things
I mean. What I want to speak about
is the humus of lives, how flesh falling
apart takes with it that last fish story,
myth made personal, and the very thighs
necessary to love. Whole days I think about
the strata of small things: gesture of a forearm
that whispered despair, a back bent over pasque flowers.
They go one by one into earth. A woman feels
that this dear head on her chest will be dear
forever—lie of the flesh! Our bodies know
we need eternity, and they breed it.
I am working at making the small things smaller.
Each day I tell myself: a smile, the brush
of an elbow will not bring happiness.
I have nothing and can remember nothing.
I close my eyes: dazzling whiteness.
Whiteness folds into whiteness and I feel
myself rising or falling. At the end
of this corridor, a door opens.

ABOUT WOMEN

Hunched over his dinner, he asks me
about women, gulps his glass of wine,
calls for more bread. He seems
to be growing bigger, maybe the food
is working; his shadow swells on the wall
behind us, looming over our heads
and the candled table. He repeats,
"Why do women ask for love?"

Face livid, he spits seed into the ashtray.
"For me," he says, "sex comes first,
and then maybe something like love."
He reaches out and breaks the wishbone:
"I'd like to make women understand
men today cannot love—if men
ever could." Behind him his shadow
is growing floppy and fat, blurred.
In a minute, he will lick my hand.

❦

SATURDAY MATINEE

Gene Autry galloping hard on his pony,
in black and white, the ground and bushes gray,
toward gray mountains under a gray sky
where white clouds drift, hooves pounding
in the small theater as I sat forward
in my seat, my heart in my mouth with envy,
with longing for freedom, for Gene Autry,
the boy beside me sliding his hand over
for mine, the odor of popcorn in place

of sagebrush, and I saw myself inside
that movie, black hat on my head while
I rushed after him, my pony dapple-gray,
my hair long and blown back by the wind,
galloping so hard but upright western style,
a real cowgirl, and the hand in the theater
like some kind of insect I was brushing away,

my body wanting to rush after my mind—
away from that kid in his button-down shirt,
away from the white clapboard houses,
the dark deciduous forest on the edges
of town, the asphalt, the street lights,
and my father forbidding me to go
to the movie while I sobbed, sobbed
for love of Gene Autry, for love
of the wide open west, of horses
and galloping, for love, for love.

THE HORSES

Every night now
for a month
I have run away
to the blue lake
where the wild horses
come to drink.

I talk to my clumsy hands.
I scold my feet.
I hide
and watch the horses,
calling their names softly,
names I invent.

"Here, Thunder Cloud!
Here, Swan Neck!"
The first time, they run away.
The second, they snort
and drink quickly,
twitching their ears.

Now they stiffen,
lift their necks
and look at me.

In the moonlight
the white coats appear blue
and the bays shadows.
In the bushes
I stand perfectly still.

My hands pry
the branches apart.
I take a step or two forward,
my skin silky, quivering.

❦

III

FAULT-FINDING

Even now the ground is slowly shifting
beneath your feet. Even now
zones of weakness are building
behind your back, ready to crack
into fractures. Even now pressures
may exceed the power of rocks
to resist. Think of it:
thousands of faults lace this region.
You live inside a ring of fire
where walls can loom up overnight.
Forces in this landscape
are trying to rearrange your world.
You stand here feeling
you can control nothing,
at any second it is you
who may be heaved up,
and broken.

❧

THE NEWS

Gus tells me about the women and children
sealed into cattle cars in Bosnia Herzegovina
in the year 1992, our year, this year,
"sent to nowhere," the TV announcer said.
Carl brings in his story of hunger
from 1952 when Europe was a sea of refugees.

The new place-mats from Venezuela,
handwoven in blue and yellow and red,
keep attracting my eye and July green
fills the windows—how lovely Colorado is!
The pilaf with its cumin and lemon juice
was *muy rico*, and the zucchini casserole—
table pleasures made keener by return
after long absence, by old friendships.

Venezuela, I have to tell them, is about
to go up. Masked students, protesting
with broken coca-cola bottles, look like
Palestinians as they throw rocks.
In Buenos Aires the Israeli embassy was blown up
and glass showered for five blocks,
decapitating pedestrians and motor bikers.

How can I come back to this silence,
to my garden full of day lilies and daisies,
blue pincushion flowers and yellow yarrow?
How can I not come back after the unbearable
tension of daily fear, the body count

each morning in *El Diario*
or its blow-by-blow account
of a beating, of a *coup de grâce*?

I come back to this ecstasy
of light, this high thin air
where we are safe,
where in this moment violence
is what we complain about on TV.

❦

SPRING IN BELGRADE

for Rivka

Gray drizzle and coal smoke, lattice
of lace curtains, new leaves spiking
outside my window—I feel chilled
to the core and achy. Black smudge
on the tenements, early risers
coughing in the weak light:
was it like this your last spring in Poland?

I think of you in Tel Aviv, Rivka,
black eyes lit by candlelight as you laughed
in the restaurant where we celebrated
your seventy years.
Your birthday arrived on a great tray:
bavarian cream drizzled with chocolate,
dazzling with blue candles
and silverfoil streamers.

I can still hear you
telling me how,
after your sister
lost her children to the ovens,
she tried to fling herself
into the electric wire.
Each time her body refused.
Rivka, there is so much
you haven't told me,
that you will never tell me.

I watched you earlier that day,
your hair, white and silky,
combed tight into a bun,
your stride proud as you led me,
a little wobbly in your too high heels,
toward the museum of the Holocaust.

Rivka, I pace on the old rampart every day.
Not far from here, early one spring,
Nazis cut two holes
in the ice on the river
and marched the old women
and children in.

When I look down from Kalamegdan fortress,
lights flicker in the black
depths of the Danube,
and I remember the tiny lights in your eyes.

❦

CITYSCAPE

You'll always arrive at this same city.
                                          —Cavafy

This city where they raped and beat you
till your face was shapeless, so swollen the technician
couldn't even x-ray you. What was your crime?
Walking along the highway at night because your car
broke down? Being a woman?

Yes, you had arrived at this same city, the city
you always seemed to return to, going around
in a circle, and those men had no known motive,
belonged to no death squad. Why did you return?
The buildings were the same concrete

as other cities'. No one ever seemed
to clean the paper-littered streets,
and the park grass had been plucked
by geese. Impossible to sit down.
Well, you had no other home.

Everything you touched fell apart,
yet you hadn't damaged it and you couldn't mend it.
Now what is left? The police wait at your bedside
to ask you who did it, when, how, why.
Your voice breaks through the bandages:

What city is this? Who did they think I was?

BREAK DANCING

Waiting for what I want to know to become clear,
I try to hone my hearing,
test the stillness settling over the streets,
but I cannot ignore
this century's bleaching of affect—I think
someone called it—lobotomy without a lobotomy,
a calm that is dead, not peaceful.
Not unlike the surgery to remove the clitoris
so women could achieve orgasm only through coitus.

But that was then. We no longer believe the womb
wanders, though a student told me his research
on lobotomy revealed women are treated with it
more often than men. Rage, rage, is no advice given us.
But where was I? It's difficult to know who one is,
even after a lifetime of saying "I."
After a lobotomy, a woman's memories no longer hurt her,
for the past was her sickness and now she will live
fixed in the eternal present.

Of course the past is a place we can never recover, not
wholly anyway. Were we all abused children?
Today we have multiple personalities, most of them
female. A doctor in Wyoming fucked his patients
as they lay on his table awaiting the speculum,
and the townspeople take his side even now.
Today we have junk mail, memos no one reads,
artificial intelligence, computers
with long memories—what are we storing inside?

Sometimes I try to remember the sea that covered our world—
the little white shells of sea snails
I found on Goat Hill and the fossils of fish bones in rocks
I brought back from the desert—and I long
for the clarity we lost with that lobe,
no matter how tenuous, and for the waves of that sea
with their undertow to pull me down into pulsing love.

❧

SHADOWS

Sarajevo

From the high hotel room in this foreign city,
I can see nearby tile roofs, chimneys, TV antennae,
and in the distance a green hill with cottages.
Inside those cottages citizens are lined up
watching *Dynasty* and *Dallas*, as the call for prayer
sails out into the evening air.

All day long they have tended shop in the bazaar,
haggling over pounded brass and copper, filigree
bracelets and earrings, or have given up treasures
to tourists trying to find a common language.

Then they have come home through the half light,
feeling like shadows of their former selves, feeling
as if they have brought with them the press
of hands, the burden of words.

Something scampers over the roof, or rustles
against their windows, and they feel tired
to death, their eyes unable to focus; the TV
sucks them in as if to take their lives
inside the box, and the shadows moving across
the screen are their inner lives.

It is their hands on her breast, their mouths
on her lips wet and red as blood; her unveiled
eyes make them look around to see
who else is there, who else is watching how her body

responds, who is envying them this blonde
totally unlike the local girls in the free swing
of her hips and the knowing look in her eyes.
They wish they could split like cells
so they could take her and still be clean.

KNIVES AND SCISSORS

Knives and scissors I'd hid
stayed in my own heart for years,
cutting away at the core.
Sometimes I felt
pruned to a new simplicity,
sometimes my heart was a sieve
letting the world in.
On the train for the south
of Chile, I had to patch up
the holes and wrap
the cloak of my flesh tight.
Slow night as we descended
the long spine of the Andes
toward ox carts and drizzle,
toward the moist foliage,
toward starlessness, and I felt
my heart opening to danger,
desire. Blank as the sky
waiting for planets. And then
the first light. The train,
slowly chugging past lean-tos,
clicked to a halt in the station
and we lugged our bags out,
mist rising over a dank pond nearby.
Cattails sharp and silver in the first light
vied with the steeples,
knives and scissors all out there.

❦

ESCAPE

How the animal shuts down,
cowering on the trail,
body hunched and flattened.
Like a lizard cornered
on the hot shale
who becomes the landscape.

And the humiliation of the hand
that reaches out to pat.
And the soul folding smaller and smaller
trying to hide, to become
rock or river.

❦

MOVING ON

I would live by the hope of moving on.
—Czeslaw Milosz

I wanted each passing season to mark me
with its colors, the wisdom of yellow,
the greater wisdom of green.

Between the seasons
I bustled, always in the direction
of winter, away from cities
into a countryside
that I passed through
as a traveler.

And now I have come
to this season of red-golds,
late autumn flickering, flaring up
in my own backyard.

Finches flitter to the feeder.
Squirrels leap across
the pruned ashes, complaining that
what they loved has been cut away.
How hard it's been
to focus on these leaves
slowly changing color.

And that is why I will
move on—I need the light
falling across the polished leather
of banana leaves and the opened
petals of orchids caught in branches.
I need the pins and needles of saguaro.

Then I can see! Then
I will be able to train
my ear so that I can hear
the barely audible rustle
and the all but weightless footfall
as I am summoned home.

❧

IV

FINDING WILD BEES ON MY SISTER'S FARM
NEAR BALTIMORE, OHIO

The swarm of bees droops from the apple tree
in a ripe pear shape, deep brown,
an angry buzzing under the damp bough.
But, the beeman says, their bellies
are so full of honey, you can pick them up
and take them home to your hive.
Hold the box for me, please.

How must it be to gather that buzzing
into its own box, closing the lid
on the deep pear of the swarm, queen
in the center and the drones
clinging in their multitude
to her homing instinct,
her sex?

The blossom-pink branch bends
from that angry weight. The moist air
lies heavy with dew and heat, spring
coming on like a bitter wreck.
My body puffy with humidity,
with jet lag, is dark with its own sting,
its own brown honey.

❦

VISITING MY SISTER

Rolling out pastry for rhubarb pie,
I argue with my sister about prayer
in the schools. Outside, rain-spotted tulips
droop, dropping the orange tears
of their petals. I ask, "It's always
Christian, isn't it?," and she says, "Well,
maybe some kid will feel what it is to be
good." We'd started to raise our voices
when suddenly I remembered how hard

I tried to be good in the way I thought
was good, struggling to obey the ten
commandments, not masturbating much.
After I read Ben Franklin I kept a diary
like his with dots on a chart for my sins
but they didn't seem to decrease, the ones
for pleasuring myself even increased,
and I would lie awake thinking how bad I was.
Late afternoons I'd go down the hill
to talk to Mrs. Duberstein about her kosher
kitchen and she showed me the second
set of everything she kept, spotted with dust.

So my mind drifts back to the pie crust
I am rolling out, the rain droning
on the roof, the swelling buds
of the iris, the Lord's Prayer
in the schools, and how it was
to be little and bad in the springtime,

pulling the flowers from the snapdragons
to examine their spotted throats,
kneeling down behind the bushes.

❦

COWS

The throaty moaning of the neighbor's cows
floats over Ohio fields;

these cows cannot be Mondrian's cows, immovable,
sketched by moonlight in his early years,

cows standing in Dutch meadows beside houses
with dead windows,

cows he called "objects of ordinary vision,"
judging his paintings worthless.

His early "Windmill in Sunlight" shrugs off its agony
in swirls of reds, yellows, blues—

as he shrugged off his when he told women
not to bring flowers, to marry someone their own age,

while he kept a tulip, an artificial one,
in a vase in his studio, its leaf painted white

because he hated
green. In the spring he chose the chair in the sidewalk cafe

that turned its back on the trees in the park.
His later paintings were dance without sex,

long expanses of white divided and crossed
by black lines too narrow to be paths.

Mondrian worked with a set square and charcoal,
erasing his trail with a pigeon's wing.

When no one wanted his work,
he talked of becoming a waiter.

But here in Ohio the cows' sad lowing floats to me—
how can it be ordinary?

In the moonlight the fields I know are green
glow white and the trees droop white leaves.

I feel the blood surging in my throat,
the sickening stumble in my breast where my heart is stuck,

a little moon lurching across my inner night:
that windmill! the bright geometry of art!

❦

LOOKING AT THE GRASS

Leaves of it! blades of it!
cover this mountain meadow with its multiple species:

reeds throw off sleepy feathers of dust-green seeds, stalks
lift up tight-packed
green sparklers, stems hoist
small tufts, almost black, pollen-flocked.

(A sea of shifting greens,
but still a garden.)

Wind scythes the field, lightening the green,
darkening it.
Shadows surge overhead.
White curdle of clouds hunkers down
above this meadow
while to the north
a dark updraft glides over the granite peak
towards me, and I feel that shiver
I felt last winter in San Bernardo de Itapa
when I tramped
to the clearing where clusters
of gray shacks
trailed plastic diapers and bottles.

The next day as our boat
glided over the Orinoco our guide suddenly slipped it
out of gear, nudged
between branches, and we were off
the river.

Among thin towering trees,
decaying branches: a sepia darkness,
water the color of weak coffee,
below and in front of us
down a narrow funnel of green.

As I stared at the water,
I grabbed the boat's gunnels:
in the water's mirror
tree tops rose under me.
When the boat picked up speed,
I was flying
upside down.

❦

STILL LIFE

for Sandy

Remember those old paintings—
piles of fruit, dead game spread out,
one duck with its head falling over the table edge—
something more than a feast.

There was lushness in those colors—
fat red and yellow apples, globes of black grapes, and then
the iridescent green of that neck
so soft your fingers itched as you stared.

And the sheen, a dusty
shine, like the one on your hair in this light.
May I stroke it?

Have you thought how dirt has crept
into the cracks of the paint in those pictures,
how it's been muting the edges of things?

We could wash the surface
but the dirt left on the cloth
would be a part of what we've been seeing:
Is it a patina of cells the living have thrown off?
Lean closer.

What we keep trying to see clearly
keeps saying: the blur, the smear, the blear,
the whole sensual conglomeration of the world.

I don't mind that aging softens everything.
Hold out your hand.
We can't look like the photos in *Vanity Fair*
or talk like the people in *People*.

Sometimes when I suddenly notice the blue and red
of my dusty tapestry on the wall
I think it glows in the late afternoon light,
lifts from its frame and floats.

Dangerous—to see you suddenly stripped of your flaws
but still you,
beautiful as all things on earth can be
when they flash before fading.

❦

SWIMMING

Say nothing for a while with a voice of
elsewhere in this
extended hereness. . . .

—Judith Herzberg

Walking along the trail into the mountains
I was startled by the sudden glint of mica
in rocks, and my heart lurched back
into the here and now, faint rustle of aspen,
high clean air, the light between trees
falling quilted onto sparse grasses.
My lungs gasped. . . . No, no, I *haven't*
told you how it was: The air smelled green.
The aspens' scarred bark was a gnarled black
against mottled gray. A blue jay! Yellow turf
springing underfoot. And. But. I'm
having trouble with my words: My motion
through stillness, a certain light: like
swimming. I moved and the world held still.
As if this place were an aquarium.
Not part of the immense Rocky Mountains.
No! It was the light's shifting.
As if blown. Something like a shudder.
Out there? I've stopped. Listen. You
can't hear the news. How many ranges
away—the fighting of Kurd guerillas?
A battered child? I pull the air
with my arms, I'm bucking. Into, out of
light? Toward.

ACKNOWLEDGMENTS

Grateful acknowledgment is made to the editors of the following magazines and anthologies in which some of these poems or earlier versions of them first appeared:

Artful Dodge: "Finding Wild Bees on My Sister's Farm Near Baltimore, Ohio" and"My Egypt";
Central Park: "Layers";
The Chattahoochee Review: "Shadows";
Eleventh Muse: "Visiting My Sister";
Graham House Review: "Moving On";
High Plains Literary Review: "Cows";
The Journal: "A Mother's Insomnia";
The Louisville Review: "Gypsy in Chinatown, Lima, Peru";
Many Mountains Moving: "As If" and "Still Life";
Nebraska Review: "The Twins Visit a Farm";
Nimrod: "Knives and Scissors";
Pacific Review: "Break Dancing";
Poetry East: "Green Wine";
The River Styx: "Cityscape";
Toyon: "About Women";
Vernal: "Hitch Hiker at a Truck Stop."

"The Horses" appeared as "Rain-in-the-Face" in *Pursuits*, edited by Jane Christensen (Scott, Foresman, and Co., 1983). "Fault-Finding" appeared in *The Forgotten Language: Contemporary American Poets and Nature*, edited by Christopher Merrill (Peregrine Smith Books, 1991). "Shadows" was reprinted in *The Chattahoochee Review Anthology* (Chattachoochee Review Press, 1995).

"The Gift" by Jorge Teillier, in my own translation, was reprinted by permission of Wesleyan University Press (University Press of New England) from *From the Country of Nevermore: Poems by Jorge Teillier*, translated by Mary Crow.

My special thanks to the Fulbright Commission for a creative writing fellowship to the former Yugoslavia and for supporting my research in Chile, Peru, Argentina, and Venezuela, which gave me memories I will never forget. Thanks also to the National Endowment for the Arts for a poetry fellowship that allowed me to travel to Greece, Israel, and Egypt; to the College of Liberal Arts, Colorado State University and Dean Loren Crabtree, for grants that have allowed me to travel widely in Latin America; to my Fort Collins poetry group—Melissa, Veronica, Lisa, and Kathy—for their support; and to my long distance poetry correspondents Mary and Marilyn for reading and commenting on so many poems.

The lines from "it's over a(see just," copyright 1944, © 1972, 1991 by the Trustees for the E. E. Cummings Trust, from *Complete Poems: 1904–1962*, by e. e. cummings, Edited by George J. Firmage. Reprinted by permission of Liveright Publishing Corporation.

"To Raj Rao," from *The Collected Poems by Czeslaw Milosz*. Copyright © 1988 by Czeslaw Milosz. First published by The Ecco Press in 1988. Reprinted by Permission.

Excerpt from "Marching" by Charles Simic. *Dismantling the Silence*, copyright © 1971 by Charles Simic. Reprinted by permission of George Braziller, Inc.

Excerpt from "Quartz Mica Feldspar," by Judith Herzberg, from *But What: Selected Poems*, translated by Shirley Kaufman and Judith Herzberg, copyright © 1988 by Oberlin College Press, reprinted by permission of Oberlin College Press.

Excerpt from *The Eiffel Tower and Other Mythologies*, by Roland Barthes, translated by Richard Howard, copyright © 1979 by Farrar, Straus & Giroux, Inc. Reprinted by permission of Hill & Wang, a division of Farrar, Straus & Giroux, Inc.

Excerpt from "The City" in *The Complete Poems of Cavafy*, copyright © 1961 and revewed 1989 by Rae Dalven, reprinted by permission of Harcourt Brace & Company.

ABOUT THE AUTHOR

Mary Crow grew up horse-crazy in Loudonville, Ohio, an identical twin in a family of eight children. Her mother was educated in art and her father was an amateur photographer; her twin, Martha, is a painter and her younger sister, Nancy, a quilter. Educated at the College of Wooster, Indiana University and the Iowa Writers Workshop, Crow moved west with her two young sons after a divorce to teach creative writing at Colorado State University. Two chapbooks of poems, *Going Home* and *The Business of Literature*, appeared in 1979 and 1980. In 1989 she published her first full-length collection of poems, *Borders*, with an introduction by David Ignatow. Her awards for poetry include a Poetry Fellowship from the National Endowment for the Arts and a Fulbright Creative Writing Fellowship; she has been named a Fellow at the White Rivers Writers Workshop and a Scholar at Breadloaf as well as held residencies at Miskenot Sha'ananim and Ragdale. She has also published three books of translations, *Woman Who Has Sprouted Wings: Poems by Contemporary Latin American Women Poets* (Second Edition, 1988), *From the Country of Nevermore: Poems by Jorge Teillier* (1990), and *Vertical Poetry: Recent Poems by Roberto Juarroz* (1992) which won a Colorado Book Award.

During her years in Colorado, Mary Crow has managed a herd of cattle, camped on the mud flats of the Colorado River, and canoed through Canyonlands National Park. Many of her poems were inspired by her trips to Spain, France, Italy, Morrocco, the former Yugoslavia (on a Fulbright Creative Writing Fellowship), Israel, Turkey, Greece, Egypt, Thailand as well as extensive travel throughout South America (with Fulbrights to Chile and Peru, Argentina, and Venezuela), where she has explored the deserts of the far north and the glaciers of the far south of both Chile and Argentina as well as the Amazon jungle in Colombia, Brazil, and Venezuela. She has also traveled to England, where she studied Shakespeare in Stratford-on-Avon. When she's home, she gardens, hikes, reads, and plans her next trip.

❦

BOA EDITIONS, LTD.
AMERICAN POETS CONTINUUM SERIES

Vol. 1   *The Führer Bunker: A Cycle of Poems in Progress*
W. D. Snodgrass

Vol. 2   *She*
M. L. Rosenthal

Vol. 3   *Living With Distance*
Ralph J. Mills, Jr.

Vol. 4   *Not Just Any Death*
Michael Waters

Vol. 5   *That Was Then: New and Selected Poems*
Isabella Gardner

Vol. 6   *Things That Happen Where There Aren't Any People*
William Stafford

Vol. 7   *The Bridge of Change: Poems 1974–1980*
John Logan

Vol. 8   *Signatures*
Joseph Stroud

Vol. 9   *People Live Here: Selected Poems 1949–1983*
Louis Simpson

Vol. 10   *Yin*
Carolyn Kizer

Vol. 11   *Duhamel: Ideas of Order in Little Canada*
Bill Tremblay

Vol. 12   *Seeing It Was So*
Anthony Piccione

Vol. 13   *Hyam Plutzik: The Collected Poems*

Vol. 14   *Good Woman: Poems and a Memoir 1969–1980*
Lucille Clifton

Vol. 15   *Next: New Poems*
Lucille Clifton

Vol. 16   *Roxa: Voices of the Culver Family*
William B. Patrick

Vol. 17   *John Logan: The Collected Poems*

Vol. 18   *Isabella Gardner: The Collected Poems*